Handling Step Functions Execution Failures

Table of Contents

1. Introduction 1

2. Understanding AWS Step Functions 2

    2.1. AWS Step Functions: Overview 2

    2.2. Interaction with AWS Services 2

    2.3. Execution Details 3

    2.4. Built-in Error Handling 3

    2.5. Utilizing AWS Step Functions: Key Benefits 3

    2.6. Securing AWS Step Functions 4

3. Identifying Execution Failures in Step Functions 5

    3.1. Understanding Step Function States 5

    3.2. Using CloudWatch Logs 6

    3.3. Understanding Error Fields 6

    3.4. Use of Dead-Letter Queues (DLQ) 7

4. The Intricacies of Execution States in Step Functions 8

    4.1. Task States 8

    4.2. Choice States 9

    4.3. Wait States 9

    4.4. Fail States 9

    4.5. Succeed States 10

    4.6. Parallel States 10

    4.7. Map States 10

5. Case Studies: Real-world Step Functions Execution Failures 12

    5.1. Case Study 1: Input Validation Failure 12

    5.2. Case Study 2: Lambda Task Timeout 13

    5.3. Case Study 3: Poor State Machine Design 13

6. Diagnosis: Tracing the Sources of Execution Failures 15

    6.1. Initialization Failures 15

    6.2. Task Failures 15

6.3. Failure due to State Machine Definition 16

6.4. Failure due to AWS Service Limits 16

6.5. Timeout Failures 17

7. Mitigation Strategies for Common Execution Failures 18

7.1. Identifying Failed Executions 18

7.2. Handling Exceptions within Task States 18

7.3. Addressing Service Failures And Timeouts 20

7.4. Implementing Execution Rollbacks 21

7.5. Designing Fail-Safe Workflows 21

7.6. Proactive Monitoring and Alerting 22

8. Best Practices to Avoid Execution Failures 23

8.1. Proper Error Handling with Retry and Catch 23

8.2. Timeout Provisions 24

8.3. Thorough Testing 25

8.4. Workflow Design 25

8.5. Limit Management 26

8.6. Regular Audits 26

9. Testing Procedures to Unearth Potential Failures 28

9.1. The Importance of Sufficient Testing 28

9.2. Establishing a Good Testing Environment 28

9.3. Developing Detailed Test Cases 29

9.4. Monitoring and Troubleshooting 29

9.5. Periodical Review and Update of Testing Strategies 30

9.6. Automating Testing 30

10. Scaling Safely: Advanced Techniques to Handle Failure 31

10.1. Identifying Failures in Step Functions 31

10.2. Handling Failures Through Retries & Catchers 32

10.3. Advanced Techniques To Preempt Failure 33

11. Staying Ahead: Monitoring and Alerting on Execution Failures . 35

11.1. Monitor Execution Failures with CloudWatch 35

11.2. Set Alert with Amazon SNS 36

11.3. Automatic Retries and Catching Failures 36

11.4. Deep Dive with CloudWatch Logs 37

11.5. Evaluate and Optimize Regularly 37

Chapter 1. Introduction

In the realm of AWS serverless services, Step Functions play a transformative role, simplifying multi-tiered, long-running tasks with various components into understandable and visually manageable flows. But what happens when these managed orchestrations descend into a realm of failure and dysfunction? Our Special Report navigates this intricate landscape, offering a detailed guide on how to expertly handle Step Functions execution failures. With a pragmatic and grounded voice, this comprehensive data-driven document delves into potential problems, mitigation strategies, and, vitally, prophylactic measures. Whether you're a seasoned AWS proponent seeking to elevate your practices or a newcomer striving to grasp the complexities, this indispensable report empower you to confidently navigate and overcome Step Functions execution failures.

Chapter 2. Understanding AWS Step Functions

AWS Step Functions provide a fully managed state-machine-based workflow execution service that enables developers to design and execute distributed algorithms and workflows for cloud applications. This chapter takes an exhaustive look at Step Functions, deconstructing its structure and components while elucidating its numerous advantages.

2.1. AWS Step Functions: Overview

Step Functions model your application as a state machine, including its components represented as states (for example, tasks or choice states). State transitions are triggered through Output and Next state properties, establishing the application's progression from one state to the next based on the output of previous tasks.

Utilizing JSON-based Amazon States Language (ASL), users define the state machine's structure and components. The ASL can document WAIT states, PARALLEL states, BRANCH states, and more. Furthermore, it specifies the conditions which lead to state changes.

2.2. Interaction with AWS Services

Step Functions seamlessly interact with a wide range of AWS services. Most notably, they can effortlessly coordinate direct service-to-service interactions, such as triggering a Lambda function or initiating an AWS Batch job. Hence, functions allow developers to adapt their applications to leverage the extensive capabilities of AWS services fully.

2.3. Execution Details

In Step Functions' parlance, execution corresponds to an instance of your state machine. It's a realization of the workflow described by your state machine's structure. Notably, Step Functions store the execution history that can be helpful to debug and traverse the execution path later.

Each run, or 'execution' as termed by AWS, progresses through states until it either successfully completes, fails, or is deliberately terminated. Here, AWS imposes a limit on total state transitions per execution, which currently stands at 25,000 transitions.

2.4. Built-in Error Handling

One of Step Functions' most notable features is its robust error handling capabilities. The conditions under which a Step Function can be directed to catch and handle errors or retry the task is defined by JSON-based ASL. For instance, retry blocks determine the circumstances of a retry, while catch blocks dictate failure handling.

Most notably, these built-in error handling and retry capabilities can significantly decrease the amount of manual error handling required in your code, simplifying the process and increasing overall resilience.

2.5. Utilizing AWS Step Functions: Key Benefits

The use of Step Functions brings several key benefits. It helps in creating and coordinating microservices that form part of your applications. By coupling visuals with code, the Step Functions Console provides a consistent, clear view of the components and flow of your application.

Its robust error handling capacities naturally promote building resilient applications. You can handle AWS service exceptions, HTTP and SQL errors, and other mishaps, right there in your state machine definition. This can result in simpler, less awkward, and robust programs.

Moreover, by enabling easy orchestration across multiple services, Step Functions can run code, store data, perform analytics, send notifications, and much more. Such actions are coordinated according to chain of precedents, making the entire execution reliable and easy to monitor with less effort.

2.6. Securing AWS Step Functions

AWS Step Functions, like other AWS services, is secured under AWS IAM service which ensures controlled and managed access. The service works on shared responsibility model. AWS takes care of security of the cloud while security in the cloud is customers' responsibility.

Step Functions also support IAM role trust policy and IAM service policy for better permission construction which can define who or what can assume the role, and what actions can be performed on the function respectively.

AWS security loves granularity, and Step Functions is no exception. From allowing execution level access to state machine ARN level access, security can be controlled at a granular level.

In conclusion, AWS Step Functions can play an invaluable role when designing and implementing intricate, complex, and long-running cloud-based workflows. While the potential for complications - including execution failures - is undeniable, Step Functions' structure and built-in error handling capabilities mean that with a carefully considered approach, these risks can be mitigated effectively.

Chapter 3. Identifying Execution Failures in Step Functions

Large-scale, serverless, and orchestrated processes offer immense transformative power, but they do not alleviate the necessity to monitor and diagnose failures. Despite the advantages of AWS Step Functions in managing long-running multi-tiered tasks, understanding how to recognize, diagnose, and resolve execution failures remains critically essential.

One of the first steps in identifying any failure is understanding the signals that may indicate a problem. Fortunately, AWS Step Functions provide various mechanisms to assist in identifying execution failures.

3.1. Understanding Step Function States

At the core of Step Functions are the individual states, each representing a single unit of work in an application. A state can be categorized either as a task, a choice, a waiter, or a parallel, among others.

Each state reports its own status. If it reports "SUCCEEDED," then that task within the workflow completed successfully. If it reports "FAILED," then that task has encountered some errors during its execution. To identify a failure, you must examine each state within a failed execution, noting any states that report a "FAILED" status.

Additionally, in the Step Functions console, the visualization graph showcases the paths that your state machine execution took. The path turns red if an error occurred, assisting you in identifying the state that failed.

3.2. Using CloudWatch Logs

AWS Step Functions integrates with Amazon CloudWatch Logs, giving a detailed performance view and insight into the behavior of your Step Functions. When an execution fails, relevant details become available in the CloudWatch Logs.

You can set up your Step Functions to send execution event data to CloudWatch Logs, which gives you a complete, chronological, ordered set of events for each execution. Each execution will have a corresponding log stream with events ordered by the time they occurred.

You can examine these logs to pinpoint the exact moment where the failure occurred. The logs will show data included in the execution event such as input, output, and the exact error message, providing key information to diagnose the failure.

Remember to set up your IAM Roles correctly to allow Step Functions to send logs to CloudWatch.

3.3. Understanding Error Fields

When a task in Step Functions fails, it provides an error field and a cause field in the output. The error field is a string that identifies the error occurred, while the cause field provides more detailed information about the error.

Taking time to understand different errors that may occur can guide the debugging process and may even guide to solutions directly.

3.4. Use of Dead-Letter Queues (DLQ)

AWS Step Functions allow the setup of Dead-Letter Queues (DLQs) which are handy in catching unhandled errors. Any error captured in this mechanism implies a failure in the overall execution process. By analyzing the errors collected in DLQs, one can comprehend the nature of the failures that may occur. Thereby, DLQs serve as an effective tool for identifying execution failures.

It is crucial to ensure your Step Functions state machine is designed with failure in mind, using the various tools and strategies at your disposal. Recognizing potential failure signals and understanding your tools can significantly reduce diagnosis time when encountering execution failures.

Understanding and recognizing failure in AWS Step Functions is not just about handling those failures when they arise, it's an opportunity to improve the design and functionality of your application. Assessment methodologies can help you perceive risk and learn from it, steering you in the proper direction for establishing robust, reliable workflows. Implementing appropriate error handling models is key to ensure your system is resilient and intelligent enough to identify and mitigate failures automatically.

In the following chapters, we delve deeper into mitigation strategies and prophylactic measures to help you handle Step Functions execution failures. Remember that comprehending the nature of the failures can often provide insights into system performance and design optimization, equipping you with the knowledge to grasp the intricacies of AWS Step Functions.

Chapter 4. The Intricacies of Execution States in Step Functions

Like every sequence of operations, AWS Step Functions consist of discreet elements—states—that come together to form a comprehensive workflow. Each state takes on a specific role in the overall execution chain, executing a task, determining which step to take next, or even stopping an execution entirely. Congruently, this evaluation of execution states aids in properly navigating potential pitfalls therein.

First, let's explore the different flavors of states in AWS Step Functions to foster a lucid understanding of their peculiar and distinct behaviors.

4.1. Task States

Our journey into execution states begins with the task state. Task states represent a single unit of work in a state machine. Typically, they are responsible for doing the actual processing. The task might be invoking a Lambda function, pausing the state machine, or even calling other AWS services.

Task responses are straightforward, once a task completes, it returns a result. However, problems arise when tasks fail. If a Lambda function exhausts its allocated memory or times out, it results in a task state failure. Also, failures occur due to insufficient IAM permissions required to execute a task or inadequate configurations. Careful attention to detail in designing IAM policies, setting suitable configurations, and handling exceptional conditions can help mitigate task state failures.

4.2. Choice States

Choice states enable decision-making ability in a state machine. A choice state evaluates a set of rules against the input and, based on that evaluation, decides the next state. It adds conditional logic to your state machine execution paths.

However, exceptions can occur if choice states have erroneous rule configurations. An exception throws when the choice state doesn't match any of the specified branches. To avoid this, include a default rule that ensures there's always a valid transition to another state when none of the conditions matches.

4.3. Wait States

Wait states provide a time delay, allowing other components to complete their processing or ensuring certain conditions are met before continuing the execution. Wait states can either delay for a specified time period or until a specific timestamp.

Issues with wait states usually arise from incorrect configuration—like providing an invalid timestamp or waiting for an unrealistic duration. Cross-checking and validating these configurations can address such hurdles.

4.4. Fail States

Designed to end the state machine execution in error, fail states allow you to define a cause and an error. They are most useful when you want to capture and handle faults in your application flow.

Since fail states are designed to fail, the occurrence of error is expected. However, careful orchestration could minimize the necessity to initiate a fail state. By adopting robust error handling and retry mechanisms in other state types, the workflow will be less likely to terminate in a fail state.

4.5. Succeed States

Identical to the fail state in terms of terminating the state machine but with an added advantage of indicating successful completion, succeed states provide a clean closure to the state machine.

A common misconception is that a successful state machine execution is equivalent to a successful execution of all tasks. However, remember, execution can reach a succeed state without executing all previous tasks— courtesy of choice states. A thorough review of the state machine design can prevent unexpected surprises.

4.6. Parallel States

Parallel states allow you to execute multiple branch start states simultaneously. Upon completion of all branches, the state machine can progress—accommodating complex scenarios under the time efficiency umbrella.

While the concept is appealing, parallel states bring increased complexity and potential for misconfiguration. Because the states execute simultaneously, a failure in any branch might lead to an overall failure. A good practice is to include a catch mechanism that traps exceptions and handles them without resorting to an execution failure.

4.7. Map States

The map state, akin to a powerful 'for-each' loop, enables the processing of a list of items in parallel. Although a map state is valuable for handling bulk data, the challenge lies in error propagation. A single execution error within the map state leads to an overall failure.

To circumvent total failure, employ a catch field in the iterator to handle exceptions. On the other hand, robust input data validation could also be a proactive method to avoid propagation of errors.

By delving deep into the delicacies and intricacies of execution states in Step Functions, we can equip ourselves with informed strategies when designing, reviewing, or debugging our workflows. Even though failure in execution is inevitable, understanding the nuances of states and their failure behaviors empowers us to mitigate and manage these obstacles strategically.

Chapter 5. Case Studies: Real-world Step Functions Execution Failures

Every practitioner espouses the importance of learning from prior victories and mishaps in software deployment. In the same vein, practical examples of Step Function execution failures and their handling can offer enlightening insights and powerful learning opportunities. To dissect these sophisticated scenarios, we've selected three distinct case studies encapsulating different types of failures, ranging from input and task failures to alarming state machine design oversights.

5.1. Case Study 1: Input Validation Failure

A game development company designed a state machine where a Step Function was to coordinate the orchestration between multiple Lambda functions. Yet unexpectedly, the primary function halted at the initial step due to an InputTypeMismatch error in the first Lambda function.

The failure occurred because the input payload did not adhere to the expected format for triggers, essentially due to lack of input validation. Instead of a JSON object, raw strings were sent, leading to failure in interpretable data extraction, which resulted in the InputTypeMismatch error.

Mitigation involved updating the initial Lambda function to validate and format the incoming payload correctly. Post adjustments, a JSON object was ensured as input, eliminating the previous error and restoring normal operation.

Prophylactic measures suggest enforcing validation checks at each layer of the application architecture. Such measures cut down the chances of deployment errors due to invalid inputs.

5.2. Case Study 2: Lambda Task Timeout

An E-commerce firm utilized Step Functions to arrange several Lambda tasks to handle their order processing system. However, the Lambda task which was processing payment information ceased functioning unexpectedly. The culminating error message, 'States.Timeout', indicated function timeout.

Investigations unveiled that the execution time of the function was exceeding the set timeout period (3 seconds). Network latency and poor exception handling affected the performance, leading to timeout.

The mitigation strategy involved enhancing function performance by optimizing the code and increasing timeout limit to 10 seconds, resulting in a successful functioning of the state machine.

To prevent similar incidences, optimizing code and setting realistic timeout limits seems ideal. Proactive performance monitoring of Lambda functions can prevent surprises like unexpected timeouts from occurring.

5.3. Case Study 3: Poor State Machine Design

An AI startup utilized Step Functions to orchestrate data processing tasks, but their state machine design failed to account for failure paths. In a scenario where a data extraction task failed, the function kept retrying indefinitely, causing significant downtime.

This failure was due to the lack of correct states to manage failures within the state machine. As it was designed to continuously retry upon failure, it trapped the function in a loop.

Mitigation relied on the redesigning of the state machine to include 'Fail' states for managing task failures, plus the inclusion of exception handling.

Prophylactically, state machine designs should always include error states and use catch blocks for handling exceptions, ensuring the machine can recover or fail gracefully under any circumstances.

These case studies elucidate how Step Functions execution failures can occur and most importantly, how to address them. Some key takeaways include the importance of validating inputs, adopting realistic timeouts and performance monitoring, and creating state machine designs that anticipate failure and deal with such events gracefully. Armed with these experiences, one can navigate complex Step Function environments effectively and build even more robust systems.

Chapter 6. Diagnosis: Tracing the Sources of Execution Failures

Execution failures within Step Functions can be challenging to diagnose and manage, often requiring deep scrutiny and a holistic understanding of the infrastructure of your AWS ecosystem. Although the AWS Management Console provides tools to troubleshoot execution errors, real-world applications call for a more comprehensive understanding of the sources of these potential hiccups.

6.1. Initialization Failures

Initialization failures can occur due to several reasons, and pinpointing the exact cause is fundamental to systematically addressing the issue.

Resource Limit Exceedance: AWS enforces a specific quota on the number of executions you can initiate. If you have exceeded these quotas, you'll encounter initialization failures. It is prudent to keep a check on your resource usage to preemptively combat this issue.

Policy-Induced Failure: Initialization failures may stem from insufficient IAM roles or policies. Troubleshooting these requires a comprehensive understanding of IAM policies, identity-based policies, service-linked roles, and resource-based policies.

6.2. Task Failures

Task failures occur during the operation of Step Functions, which may dismantle the delicate orchestration of the serverless service.

Lambda Function Failures: AWS Step Functions service often incorporates the use of AWS Lambda functions. A failure may be traced back to Lambda when there's an unhandled exception within its code. This can be mitigated by ensuring error handling within Lambda functions.

Activity Failures: Activities encompass automated tasks that AWS Step Function performs. An incorrect implementation or abrupt termination can lead to failure. These need to be appropriately defined and monitored to circumvent any possible issues.

6.3. Failure due to State Machine Definition

State Machine failure is a common source of execution failures. The proper implementation, validation, and testing of State Machine definitions can prevent the operational disruption of your AWS Step Functions workflows.

Invalid Transition: If a State Machine Definition transitions to a state that doesn't exist, it immediately triggers a failure. Carefully designing and testing your State Machine can avoid this mistake.

Overuse of the Parallel State: Using too many tasks in parallel states can lead to ThrottlingException errors. Reducing the number of parallel tasks, or managing them minimally, can mitigate this issue.

6.4. Failure due to AWS Service Limits

AWS imposes service limits on various processes, such as the number of concurrent executions, number of states, and the input payload size. Continuous monitoring of your execution can avert potential issues and keep your services running smoothly.

6.5. Timeout Failures

Timeout failures occur when an execution or task exceeds the allotted time. Understanding how to configure your functions and executions to effectively manage timeouts is vital to ensure proper operation.

Execution Timeout: AWS Step Functions have an execution time limit that, when exceeded, will halt the execution. This could lead to execution failure if not appropriately managed.

Lambda Function Timeouts: If the AWS Lambda functions embedded in the Step Function exceed their set time, these functions cease their operation, thereby leading to Step Function execution failure.

These sources of Step Functions execution failures articulate the intricacies of AWS serverless services. Developing strategies to diagnose these failures enables you to craft robust and resilient AWS solutions. This chapter highlighted the most common causes of execution failures. Moving forward, we will dive deeper into these potential problems, discussing how to detect, diagnose, and address these in real-time effectively.

Chapter 7. Mitigation Strategies for Common Execution Failures

While diving into the world of AWS Step Functions, one becomes familiar with the complexities of long-running executions. There's a broad range of typical failures, primarily originating from service issues, timeouts, or exceptions within task states. Quite frequently, complex multi-service workflows may fail due to a trifling problem in a single service, which underscores the need to erect robust and effective mitigation strategies.

7.1. Identifying Failed Executions

The first step toward mitigating execution failures lies in identification. Detecting failed executions promptly and efficiently is crucial; this is where CloudWatch, AWS's monitoring and observability service, comes into play. Using CloudWatch Events, you can set up your system to respond to execution status changes. When an execution fails, CloudWatch can trigger a response, such as sending a notification or running a Lambda function to address the issue.

7.2. Handling Exceptions within Task States

A common class of failures in Step Functions executions are exceptions thrown within task states. When such tasks are coded improperly or face unusual inputs, they may fail, causing the entire execution to fail. Scenarios that typically lead to such exceptions include:

- Insufficient error handling

- Unanticipated input

- Overuse of resources

To manage these issues, the Leaky Bucket algorithm, Retry and Catch fields come in handy. The Leaky Bucket algorithm is a congestion control measure that can handle such bursts gracefully. Meanwhile, integrating retry and catch mechanisms into your task states provides a second line of defence.

The '**Retry**' field takes a list of error names that should trigger it, a maximum number of retries, an interval that determines the time to wait before the next retry, and optionally, a backoff rate. The '**Catch**' field specifies recovery paths when certain errors occur, with it catching all errors by default.

A loose 'Retry' example could resemble the following:

```
"Retry": [
  {
    "ErrorEquals": ["MyError"],
    "IntervalSeconds": 1,
    "MaxAttempts": 2,
    "BackoffRate": 2.0
  }
]
```

And a typical 'Catch' would look like:

```
"Catch": [
  {
    "ErrorEquals": ["MyError"],
    "Next": "RecoveryState"
  }
```

Implementing such exception management helps mitigate execution failures originating from task states.

7.3. Addressing Service Failures And Timeouts

While Step Functions enhance inter-service coordination, they do not eliminate service failures or latency issues. A robust execution design should cater for such eventualities. A common way to control service execution is by applying a timeout, or, in other words, specifying a duration after which if the state has not yet finished, the service ends it. An illustrative example in a Task state could be:

```
{
  "Type": "Task",
  "TimeoutSeconds": 30,
  "Resource": "arn:aws:lambda:us-east-
1:123456789012:function:HelloWorld",
  "End": true
}
```

For services that are typically susceptible to latency issues, it is recommended to incorporate redundant states along with timeouts. Another valid strategy includes setting up monitoring tools like CloudWatch, which would track the latency of inter-service calls and alert for any anomalies.

7.4. Implementing Execution Rollbacks

In certain business scenarios, execution failures might require rollbacks. AWS Step Functions have built-in integration with AWS Lambda, which allows you to execute compensating transactions or fallback actions if an execution fails. This strategy would involve:

- Creating a Lambda function that runs the compensating transaction.

- Adding a '**Catch**' field in the steps that, if they fail, should trigger a rollback, pointing to a Fail state which triggers the compensating Lambda function.

The compensating transaction should be idempotent, meaning it can run multiple times without causing unintended side effects.

7.5. Designing Fail-Safe Workflows

For significant business operations, it's vital to design Fail-safe workflows where even if an execution fails, the workflow adapts and continues to function. AWS Step Functions provide mechanisms to do this efficiently:

- '**Error handling**': As discussed earilier, 'Retry' and 'Catch' fields can help minimize task failures.

- '**Fallback states**': Fallback states act as a safety measure that regularly monitors the health of the primary task and takes over in the event of a failure.

- '**Parallel states**': Parallel states allow you to incorporate redundant tasks to add an extra level of resilience. Here, if one branch fails, the other branches can still continue.

Fail-safe workflows add another level of reliability to your Step

Functions executions, minimizing the impact of execution failures.

7.6. Proactive Monitoring and Alerting

Proactive monitoring empowers you to detect and address failures before they gravely impact your applications. AWS CloudWatch can be set up for alerting based on Step Functions metrics. You can create dashboards to have a dedicated view of all your Step Functions executions and promptly identify any failures. Setting SNS Stations for significant events like execution failures enable swift resolution of issues with service degradation or breakdown.

In conclusion, addressing Step Functions execution failures demands an intricate, layered strategy. Each layer, from careful identification and effective exception management to designing fail-safe workflows and proactive monitoring, fortifies your applications against failure scenarios. This labour is indeed a key determinant in your journey towards building scalable, resilient systems within the AWS serverless ecosystem.

Chapter 8. Best Practices to Avoid Execution Failures

The ability to effectively manage AWS Step Functions extends beyond just understanding how to deploy and operate them; it includes understanding how to avoid execution failures. Here are some best practices that any AWS practitioner can follow to minimize execution failures and improve the overall efficiency of the Step Functions service.

8.1. Proper Error Handling with Retry and Catch

One of the cardinal rules when working with Step Functions - or any system that depends on communication between multiple components - is to anticipate failures. When a failure occurs in AWS Step Functions, those failures are categorized as either handled or unhandled.

In the AWS Step Functions world, error handling is accomplished through a combination of retry and catch fields. These are defined type-specifically and can be set using various attributes including ErrorEquals, IntervalSeconds, MaxAttempts, and BackoffRate. The ErrorEquals field is especially important as it defines the list of error names that will lead to the retry or catch block initiating.

```
{
   "ErrorEquals": [ "States.ALL" ],
   "IntervalSeconds": 1,
   "MaxAttempts": 3,
   "BackoffRate": 2.0
}
```

This configuration ensures that a failed execution steps retries thrice with a base interval of 1 second between each attempt, and with a back-off rate of two.

Ensure an appropriate catch mechanism is in place with the right details from the failed states. It's advisable and a best practice to have fallback workflows or states to handle an exception gracefully.

8.2. Timeout Provisions

Every AWS Step Function has a built-in system-dictated maximum execution time poised at one year. Nevertheless, individual tasks executed within Step Functions can define their own custom timeout values to induce greater control. This intrinsic feature helps to thwart executing runaway functions that sporadically drain resources in an unrestricted fashion.

Utilize the Retry and TimeoutSeconds fields to help circumvent timeout failures. The TimeoutSeconds field is helpful to determine the maximum allowed time duration before a state is marked as failed, while the Retry field works for transient issues.

```
{
  "TimeoutSeconds": 10,
  "Retry": [
    {
      "ErrorEquals": ["States.ALL"],
      "IntervalSeconds": 1,
      "MaxAttempts": 5,
      "BackoffRate": 2.0
    }
  ]
}
```

This setting ensures that your function execution attempts to retry up to 5 times if it fails, with an interval of 1 second and a maximum attempt period of 10 seconds.

8.3. Thorough Testing

Implementing thorough testing not only ensures the accuracy of your Step Functions, but it also minimizes the probability of encountering an unexpected execution failure. Use the AWS Step Functions Console, CLI, or SDKs to synthetically induce various test cases and track response types.

Leverage the AWS Step Functions local development environment to emulate AWS Step Functions and complete services interaction, reflecting the AWS Cloud environment as accurately as possible.

AWS console allows executing states in an independent manner, individually testing them for exceptions or unforeseen errors. AWS X-ray, AWS CloudWatch metrics and logging are indispensable tools you should use for performance monitoring and efficient debugging.

True to the concept of 'prevention is better than cure', it's far easier - and cheaper - to detect and address flaws during the developmental stages, rather than remedying them in the production phase.

8.4. Workflow Design

Decisions made during the design phase can dramatically impact the overall success of your AWS Step Functions. Design your workflows for idempotency. Idempotent designs have the same result regardless of how many times it's executed after the initial attempt. This is crucial because Step Functions follow an at-least-once execution model wherein they might execute a function more than once to compensate for transient issues.

Design your Step Functions for atomicity by ensuring certain steps are executed as an indivisible unit. Break your monolithic applications into a plethora of smaller, single-responsibility actions that neatly gel within a workflow.

Embed the notion of data consistency within workflows. As AWS Step Functions inherently pass data between tasks, data consistency ensures a more robust and fail-safe system that stands guarded against silent data corruption.

8.5. Limit Management

Each AWS account has distinct per-region quotas (also known as limits) on resources, API requests, and quotas within the AWS Step Functions service. Be aware of your limits and pursue limit increments strategically to cater to the specific requirements of your applications.

Monitor your functions' executions and trends to keep an eye on the approaching service quota. The AWS Management Console provides effective mechanisms to gauge your current quota usage and to request limit increases when required.

8.6. Regular Audits

Periodical audits of your AWS Step Functions can ensure they are running in compliance with the best practices stated in this section. Make use of AWS Well-Architected Tool (AWS WA Tool) and AWS Trusted Advisor to check for any high-risk issues or gaps in your deployed Step Functions.

These best practices serve as a compass to guide you through the intricate world of AWS Step Functions, helping you build robust, reliable, and resilient Step Function workflows. By keeping an eye on service metrics, being preemptive about potential failure points, and responding rapidly to any arising issues, you can significantly reduce

Step Function execution failures and maintain your AWS environment's health and efficiency.

Chapter 9. Testing Procedures to Unearth Potential Failures

Testing and verifying your Step Functions workflows is a pivotal step to unearth any potential failures that could cause an execution flaw. It's not only about seeing it work under ideal conditions but also about ensuring it performs as expected under adverse conditions. It is an axiom that a thoroughly tested Step Function is a reliable one.

9.1. The Importance of Sufficient Testing

In any system, the importance of sufficient testing can never be underestimated. It's especially true when dealing with Step Functions. A Step Function may consist of multiple interdependent tasks, and any error in one task can break the entire chain of operations. Furthermore, some tasks may fail silently, leaving you entirely unaware of an issue unless you are specifically looking for it. Testing ensures that problems like these are caught and fixed before they can cause widespread execution failures.

9.2. Establishing a Good Testing Environment

Before you begin testing, make sure you have a good environment established. This means your testing environment should mirror production as closely as possible, but without any of the risks associated with actually making changes to production. AWS offers various options to set up separate environments, like accounts, VPCs, and namespaces.

9.3. Developing Detailed Test Cases

Test cases are an essential aspect of unearthing potential failures. You should have tests designed to ensure that every part of your Step Function is performing as expected.

1. Sequential Testing: Test each state of your Step Function individually. This type of testing is integral to troubleshooting specific issues.

2. Integrated Testing: Here, you'll test the entire function from start to finish. This kind of testing will ensure that states work together correctly.

3. Edge Testing: Push the boundaries of your Step Function. Test it under conditions where it's likely to fail to see how it behaves. This could include injecting failures, triggering retry limits, or testing with unusually large datasets.

4. Regression Testing: Any time you make changes to your Step Function, rerun your tests. This will confirm that your changes haven't introduced any new bugs.

9.4. Monitoring and Troubleshooting

Just running tests isn't enough. You need to monitor them and observe how your Step Function behaves during testing. AWS CloudWatch, AWS CloudTrail, and X-Ray services can be helpful tools to monitor Step Functions and check logs. To troubleshoot Step Function failures, use Amazon CloudWatch Logs Insights to drill down into interactions between services.

9.5. Periodical Review and Update of Testing Strategies

Finally, testing isn't a one-time affair. It demands ongoing attention and periodic reviews to capture any changes made to the Step Function over time. As you add functionality, make sure your tests continue to cover all possible edge cases.

9.6. Automating Testing

Automated testing can be a fantastic way to streamline processes and make sure nothing is overlooked. You can use AWS CodePipeline, a fully managed continuous delivery service, and AWS CodeBuild, a fully managed build service, to automate your testing routines. AWS SAM (Serverless Application Model) also lets you build, test, and debug your AWS Lambda functions on your local machines before deploying.

Testing Step Functions is an integral part of their implementation and management. Your testing strategies need to be as robust and detailed as your Step Functions themselves. By implementing the procedures mentioned above, you can find potential failures before they become real issues, ensuring smoother Step Functions execution and saving both time and resources.

Chapter 10. Scaling Safely: Advanced Techniques to Handle Failure

To truly embrace the power and reliability of AWS Step Functions, we must first accept and prepare for failures. These may arise from timeouts, errors in the code, or even hitches in downstream resources consumed by individual tasks. Despite the complexities, employing certain advanced techniques and strategies can soft-pedal these incidences. These methods ultimately enhance the efficiency and safety of your scaling practices.

10.1. Identifying Failures in Step Functions

The initial stage of handling AWS Step Functions failures lies in efficiently identifying them. Typical indicators of execution failure include:

- Explicit failure events triggered by your Lambda function or your own code. For instance, your code might call the 'Fail' State Type in an explicit Fail State, complete with an error and cause.

- Exceptions thrown within your code that aren't caught. They often signify unanticipated issues and can lead to immediate termination of the task.

- Task timeouts. If your task outlives its heartbeat or doesn't return a status after a while, Step Functions construes it as a failure.

- Retry attempts surpassing the maximum set limit.

The AWS Step Functions console neatly highlights these anomalies, flagging tasks with an 'Execution Failed' message and appending an error message and an optional Error Cause JSON payload.

10.2. Handling Failures Through Retries & Catchers

'States.Retrieve' let you set 'Retry' and 'Catch' fields to deterministically handle failure within the state.

- 'Retry' helps offset transient issues (like network glitches) by retrying the failed operation a specified number of times. It converges on step executions on idle intervals to ensure that temporary errors don't spiral into full-blown failures.

```
{
    "Retry": [
        {
        "ErrorEquals": ["States.ALL"],
        "IntervalSeconds": 1,
        "MaxAttempts": 5,
        "BackoffRate": 2.0
        }
    ]
}
```

This JSON example defines a retry policy applied to all(errors), tuned to retry after one second, a maximum of five attempts, with a backoff rate of 2, doubling the wait interval each time.

- Catchers act as your tasks' safety net. They come in handy when retries fail to salvage your executions or when certain errors need a special handler state.

```
{
```

```
  "Catch": [
    {
    "ErrorEquals": [ "States.ALL" ],
    "Next": "Recovery State"
    }
  ]
}
```

In this example, the Catch clause promises that upon any failure, execution jumps to the "Recovery state".

This technique enhances your workflow's robustness by prompting Step Functions to execute alternative states or halt execution when encountering errors.

10.3. Advanced Techniques To Preempt Failure

While retries and catchers can ameliorate the effects of some failures, preemptive strategies prove more effective in some scenarios. Here are some advanced techniques you can apply:

- Limiting Retry Attempts: While retries provide a safety net, infinite retry attempts can be a drain on resources. Limit the retry attempt to avoid redundant executions.

- Parameterizing Retry Fields: Variables can be used in the Retry field to adjust retry behavior dynamically based on external parameters or the state of your application.

- Utilizing AWS Lambda Destinations: For asynchronous Lambda invocations, use Lambda Destinations to route the execution results –success or failure– to another AWS service without involving Step Functions.

- Heartbeats for Long-Running Activities: Use the

HeartbeatSeconds field to manage long-running activities and timeout processes that do not respond within a specified period.

- Validation of Input: Validation at the inception prevents invalid inputs from catalyzing failures in subsequent tasks. Use Choice states to filter and redirect erroneous inputs.

Conclusively, preempting potential failures is a crucial aspect of scaling safely with AWS Step Functions. Leveraging the methods detailed above, you can establish resilient and durable serverless workflows ready to stand the test of time and complexity.

Chapter 11. Staying Ahead: Monitoring and Alerting on Execution Failures

In the realm of AWS Step Functions, vigilance is the foundation upon which reliable services are built. Upfront monitoring and effective alerting play a pivotal role in staying ahead, preempting and efficiently dealing with execution failures.

Let's delve into the practices that ensure we are not caught unawares by troublesome failures.

11.1. Monitor Execution Failures with CloudWatch

CloudWatch allows us to actively monitor AWS resources and applications in near real-time. With AWS Step Functions, a suite of CloudWatch metrics enables us to track state machine executions, including failures.

To observe Step Functions metrics in CloudWatch, navigate through the AWS Management Console to CloudWatch. From there, you should select 'Metrics', then 'Step Functions', and thereafter your desired state machine. Here, the 'ExecutionsFailed' metric reflects the number of executions that failed within the last minute.

Make certain that monitoring this metric becomes an immediate emphasis of your Step Functions management. This practice will enable you to rapidly identify when executions begin to falter.

11.2. Set Alert with Amazon SNS

Having useful metrics is one thing, but meaningful and timely alerts truly make the difference. Transient network blips or minor code hiccups could lead to execution failures, and it's important to act quickly in these situations. Amazon Simple Notification Service (SNS) provides a solid mechanism for accomplishing this.

To set alerts with Amazon SNS, navigate to the CloudWatch console, select the 'Alarms' tab, then 'Create Alarm'. Select 'Step Functions' under AWS Namespaces, and choose the previously highlighted 'ExecutionsFailed' metric. Configure thresholds and select 'in alarm' as the state to trigger the action, then stipulate the action as 'Send notification to...'. Enter your SNS Topic ARN, and finish by naming and creating your alarm.

This alert provides crucial visibility into any execution failures as they happen, promoting a proactive response.

11.3. Automatic Retries and Catching Failures

The raw power of AWS Step Functions lies in its intrinsic ability to handle exceptions automatically. By configuring the 'Retry' field of a state, you determine how many times Step Functions will automatically retry a state when an error occurs. The 'MaxAttempts' field can be adjusted to set the maximum number of retry attempts.

Additionally, the 'Catch' field can be utilized to divert executions to another state based on different error types. This mechanism should be designed with the anticipated failure scenarios in mind to provide the most suitable response.

Remember not to discount the fact that every failure offers a learning opportunity. Careful design and configuration of these automatic retries and catches can turn a potential catastrophe into a short-lived glitch.

11.4. Deep Dive with CloudWatch Logs

While CloudWatch metrics and alarms offer a bird's eye view of your executions, CloudWatch Logs offers a deep dive, providing an opportunity to scrutinize potential problem areas.

CloudWatch Logs records execution history events, from the start of an execution to its end. By enabling CloudWatch Logs in your state machine, you're empowered with valuable insights about the input and output of each state, transition paths, time stamps and error details.

This granular data presents a powerful tool to investigate the particulars of an execution failure, aiding immensely in diagnosing issues and implementing accurate solutions.

11.5. Evaluate and Optimize Regularly

Last, but not least, continuous improvement plays a significant role in managing Step Functions execution failures. Regular evaluation of failure occurrences, their reasons, and the effectiveness of the response mechanism ensures that your AWS Step Functions landscape remains resilient.

Establish a recurring review process to evaluate failures. Use this process not only to discuss the corrective measures but also to brainstorm preventive strategies. This will further fortify your state machines, making them resilient to failures.

The magic of AWS Step Functions lies not just in its robust orchestration capabilities, but also in its ability to cope with, and recover from failures. With a comprehensive approach towards monitoring, alerting, automatic retries, deep dive analysis, and regular optimization, you can stay well ahead of execution failures, ensuring your services remain optimal and resilient.